The Essential

VOL

700/900 SERIES

1982 to 1998

Your marque expert:
Tim Beavis

VELOCE PUBLISHING
THE PUBLISHER OF FINE AUTOMOTIVE BOOKS

Essential Buyer's Guide Series
Alfa Romeo Giulia GT (Booker)
Alfa Romeo Spider Giulia (Booker & Talbott)
Austin Seven (Barker)
Big Healeys (Trummel)
BMW E21 3 Series (1975-1983) (Reverente, Cook)
BMW GS (Henshaw)
BSA Bantam (Henshaw)
BSA 500 & 650 Twins (Henshaw)
Citroën 2CV (Paxton)
Citroën ID & DS (Heilig)
Cobra Replicas (Ayre)
Corvette C2 Sting Ray 1963-1967 (Falconer)
Ducati Bevel Twins (Falloon)
Fiat 500 & 600 (Bobbitt)
Ford Capri (Paxton)
Harley-Davidson Big Twins (Henshaw)
Hinckley Triumph triples & fours 750, 900, 955, 1000, 1050, 1200 – 1991-2009 (Henshaw)
Honda CBR600 Hurricane (Henshaw)
Honda CBR FireBlade (Henshaw)
Honda SOHC fours 1969-1984 (Henshaw)
Jaguar E-type 3.8 & 4.2-litre (Crespin)
Jaguar E-type V12 5.3-litre (Crespin)
Jaguar XJ 1995-2003 (Crespin)
Jaguar XK8 & XKR (1996-2005) (Thorley)
Jaguar/Daimler XJ6, XJ12 & Sovereign (Crespin)
Jaguar/Daimler XJ40 (Crespin)
Jaguar Mark 1 & 2 (All models including Daimler 2.5-litre V8) 1955 to 1969 (Thorley)
Jaguar XJ-S (Crespin)
Jaguar XK 120, 140 & 150 (Thorley)
Land Rover Series I, II & IIA (Thurman)
Mazda MX-5 Miata (Mk1 1989-97 & Mk2 98-2001) (Crook)
Mercedes-Benz 280SL-560DSL Roadsters (Bass)
Mercedes-Benz 'Pagoda' 230SL, 250SL & 280SL
Roadsters & Coupés (Bass)
MGA 1955-1962 (Sear, Crosier)
MGB & MGB GT (Williams)
MG Midget & A-H Sprite (Horler)
MG TD, TF & TF1500 (Jones)
Mini (Paxton)
Morris Minor & 1000 (Newell)
New Mini (Collins)
Norton Commando (Henshaw)
Peugeot 205 GTI (Blackburn)
Porsche 911 (930) Turbo series (Streather)
Porsche 911 (964) (Streather)
Porsche 911 (993) (Streather)
Porsche 911 (996) (Streather)
Porsche 911 Carrera 3.2 series 1984 to 1989 (Streather)
Porsche 911SC – Coupé, Targa, Cabriolet & RS Model years 1978-1983 (Streather)
Porsche 924 – All models 1976 to 1988 (Hodgkins)
Porsche 928 (Hemmings)
Porsche 986 Boxster series (Streather)
Porsche 987 Boxster and Cayman series (Streather)
Rolls-Royce Silver Shadow & Bentley T-Series (Bobbitt)
Subaru Impreza (Hobbs)
Triumph Bonneville (Henshaw)
Triumph Herald & Vitesse (Davies, Mace)
Triumph Spitfire & GT6 (Baugues)
Triumph Stag (Mort & Fox)
Triumph TR6 (Williams)
Triumph TR7 & TR8 (Williams)
Vespa Scooters – Classic 2-stroke models 1960-2008 (Paxton)
VW Beetle (Cservenka & Copping)
VW Bus (Cservenka & Copping)
VW Golf GTI (Cservenka & Copping)

www.veloce.co.uk

First published in May 2013 by Veloce Publishing Limited, Veloce House, Parkway Farm Business Park, Middle Farm Way, Poundbury, Dorchester, Dorset, DT1 3AR, England.
Fax 01305 250479/e-mail info@veloce.co.uk/web www.veloce.co.uk or www.velocebooks.com.

ISBN: 978-1-845844-56-1 UPC: 6-36847-04456-5

Introduction
– the purpose of this book

Originally intended as a replacement for the 240, the 700 Series began life in 1982 with the luxurious 760, which was offered with a smooth 2.8-litre V6 engine. In fact, the 240 remained in production until 1993 as a smaller option in the Volvo range. The popularity of the new 760 and reliability of the 240's four-cylinder Red Block engine then combined in 1984 with the introduction of the 740, a more affordable yet still very well equipped 700.

Around the beginning of the 1990s, the 700 Series cars were gradually replaced by the respective 900 Series counterparts, which offered a new, sleeker look and the gradual introduction of other refinements. These included the new, more refined M90 gearbox, multi-link rear suspension that had featured on 760s from 1988 onward, and a new, 24-valve straight-six petrol engine, a precursor to the five-cylinder unit used on 850s. In many markets, some of the last 960 models were rebranded as the S90 (Saloon/Sedan) and V90 (Estate/Wagon). This was a turning point for Volvo, making way for the V70 and forever changing model numbers to this

The 240 actually outlived the 700 Series.

The squared-off boot (trunk) of 700 series cars is unmistakable.

The sleeker V90s, with the smooth 24v straight six, forever changed the naming format.

new format. The new modular engines also ended the reign of the infamous Red Block, and the rear-wheel drive era was effectively over.

'Old brick,' 'big boat,' and 'lumbering tank,' are some phrases you may know of, and will hear more often once you own a 700/900 Series. However, Volvo literally means 'I roll,' and after a short time of ownership, you'll not only find yourself rolling with these minor punches, but defending your sturdy 'brick' like you would a pet or a child! That is of course only if you've bought a worthy example. Fear not, however, as this book will provide you with all you need to know to go and do exactly that.

Thanks
I would like to thank all the members and administrators of the various clubs and forums that have assisted me with this book, extending special thanks in particular to Turbobricks.com and The Volvo Owners' Club UK.

The 850 T5-R succeeded the 900 Series but never outlived it.

Adrian Tasker's V70R AWD; a rare gem born from the death of the rear-wheel drive era.

Contents

THE ESSENTIAL BUYER'S GUIDE™ CURRENCY

At the time of publication a BG unit of currency "●" equals approximately £1.00/ US$1.50/Euro 1.15. Please adjust to suit current exchange rates using Sterling as the base currency.

1 Is it the right vehicle for you?
– marriage guidance

Tall & short drivers

There's a lot of space around the driver and front passenger. Drivers of almost all sizes can be easily accommodated, as seats have generous adjustments for reach and height, with adjustable lumbar support on most models. Adjustable steering wheels were also available on later 960 models. Headroom for taller passengers is somewhat limited in the back.

Lumbar adjustment makes all the difference on longer journeys.

Headroom in the back is not plentiful but enough for the average adult.

Controls

Clutches on older models are a little heavy by modern standards, but not strenuously so. Power steering is surprisingly light for a large car of this age; one-handed manoeuvring is easy. Brakes have good modulation, even by modern standards. The four-speed gearbox with overdrive feels heavy and mechanical, with the later M90 five-speed operating more smoothly. Both units are sturdier than average, especially later M90s.

The dash and controls have a purposeful, solid feel.

Will it fit in the garage?

700 Series
Length: 4.79m
Width: 1.75m
Height: 1.43m
(petrol/gas turbo models are lower)

900 Series saloon (sedan)
Length: 4.87m
Width: 1.75m
Height: 1.41 to 1.46m
(petrol/gas turbo models are lower)

This folding bench seat increases an estate's seating capacity to seven.

900 Series estate (wagon)
Length: 4.85m
Width: 1.75m
Height: 1.46m
(petrol/gas turbo models are lower)

Not as good as split folding seats but enables you to transport long objects such as skis.

Interior space
Seats provide high levels of comfort in all trims. All models can accommodate five adults with the capacity increasing to seven seats in estates fitted with a folding bench seat. The wide linear bodies provide acres of boot space, with estates rivalling small vans. The rear seats of saloons (sedans) don't split fold but have a sliding door opening behind the centre arm rest for skis and other long objects.

Usability
There is a wide range of engines to choose from (see chapter 7 for a summary). Rear-wheel drive allows an excellent turning circle for parking and manoeuvring, a nice surprise for such a big car. Most examples take light off-roading in their stride with the right tyres. High torque and stability makes for an excellent tow vehicle. With a smooth driving style the large chassis can handle well for both leisurely, as well as spirited driving. Multi-link rear suspension available on V90, S90 and later 960 models futher improve handling.

Running costs
Cheap insurance considering the available engine power. Infamous reliability. Models with Bosch Motronic injection are more thirsty around town than newer models with Bosch Jetronic management. Fuel use and a large tank make filling up expensive, but long journeys can produce surprising fuel economy.

Parts availability
Varies with the type of part. General replacements are easily found, but with fewer and fewer examples on the road, certain parts, such as alloys and body or trim pieces, can be few and far between. Aftermarket alloy wheels can be particularly difficult to source, with a less common 5x108 PCD (pitch circle diameter) and rare offset measurement.

Investment potential
Saloon turbo models with a manual gearbox are becoming very rare and fetching high prices for their age – possibly a future classic. 780 models are already considered ultra rare classics. With many cars being used for working and as family vehicles, a well kept example should hold its value.

The very rare Volvo 780.

Plus points: High comfort and reliability. Generally strong and very well engineered in all aspects. Plenty of space and power, especially in estate and turbo models respectively. Many modern features for an older car, at little money to boot.

Minus points: Relatively high fuel consumption. Although capable, handling can take getting used to. Regarded by some as a stereotype of geriatric ownership and 'boxy' styling. 2.0-litre carburetted and non-turbo diesel engines lack power.

Alternatives
BMW 7 Series, Mercedes 190E/190D, Mitsubishi Gallant, Ford Granada, Jaguar XJ, Vauxhall Omega, Lexus LS400.

2 Cost considerations
– affordable, or a money pit?

Purchase price
Prices can vary, but within a very affordable range. One of the main attractions of purchasing a 700/900 Series Volvo is the amount of car you get for your money, both figuratively and literally.

Being at the luxury end of the market in their day, a host of extras are commonly available such as heated seats, electrically operated wing mirrors, and heating ducted through to the rear of the vehicle. Neglecting to maintain or fix these extras when they go wrong can be a major factor in lowering value. This, together with some examples having had a hard working life, has allowed sale prices to drop as low as ⬤400 in some cases. However, there are plenty of careful owners to balance this out, with vehicles for sale that would put any classic car enthusiast to shame. Such examples can fetch up to ⬤2000, and with some models such as the manual 740 Turbo Intercooler becoming increasingly rare, careful owners could see such cars fetching more with time.

Acres of load space even before the rear seats have been folded down.

Well cared for examples can hold value, such as Dustin Hulting's immaculate 740.

Running costs
Most models will see between 20 and 23mpg (Imp) around town, and 25 to 28mpg (Imp) on a run. Insurance is generally cheap due to age and image as a comfortable family cruiser. A good example will be very reliable and see costly maintenance and repair bills few and far between.

Parts prices

With a range of parts that can be fitted across models, and more sources than ever, finding most general parts is not difficult, if a bit time-consuming on occasion. However, be on the lookout for cheap spares that fail to meet standards. Volvo have a good reputation for service in this area, and whilst there are cheaper alternatives, genuine Volvo parts are almost always worth the extra money, especially when you remember that the rest of the car is likely to last a long time.

Fuel economy isn't bad, but you'll be here a while to fill the tank!

Typical costs based on a late 740:

Timing belt 11
Water pump 62
Alternator belt 9
Power steering belt 9
Water pump belt 12
Timing belt tensioner 22
Gasket kit 70
Head gasket 46
Head bolts 85

Brake pads front 16
Brake pads rear 12
Fuel pump 36
Radiator 75
Alternator 66
Starter motor 58
Front shocks (pair) 105
Rear shocks (pair) 65
Wheel bearing 15

M90 dual mass flywheel and Sachs clutch.

3 Living with a 700/900 Series
– will you get along together?

There aren't so many rear-wheel drive cars produced today, although, they do have their advantages. As well as being a general preference for driving enthusiasts, a longitudinally-mounted engine allows for cavernous wheel arches. Together with the lack of a driveshaft at the front, this provides 700/900s with an astounding turning circle. Whilst being essential for the car's large size and square frontage, this also provides a great deal of enjoyment, as it can be manoeuvred in spaces that would frustrate drivers of smaller, modern cars. This goes some way to redeem the 700/900 for its size – considered off-putting by some.

Rear wheel drive also saves paintwork –
a front wheel drive car would've thrown
this ice and debris onto the bodywork!

More badge = more power!

As well as four passengers, plenty can fit in a Saloon.

Clearly the vast amount of space that comes with these cars is what should seal the deal, feeling as big inside as they look on the outside. Putting the seats down enables the estates to swallow more than some small vans. Even the saloon, which suffers here from fixed rear seating, can fit a huge amount in the boot. In fact the only space constraint is revealed when transporting taller adults in the rear, where head room is limited by the fuel tank and axle beneath. Children, however, will not be scrabbling for views outside as they would be in most cars, and won't feel tucked away in the back.

It's details like this headlamp ventilation tube that make these such well engineered cars.

Another common criticism for 700/900s is their soft suspension and boat-like feel. This, and their aforementioned size have been one of the biggest turn-offs for some prospective buyers of the marque. The handling cannot match up to the advances in suspension geometry found on current vehicles, but in reality, adjusting one's driving style is the main obstacle. In the right hands, a 700/900 Series is surprisingly quick through the bends, yet still equally at home being driven more sedately, getting the most out of the comfort they are famed for. Performance is by no means lacking, but doesn't offer much to get the pulse racing. That is unless you opt for the 2.3 Turbo Intercooler, which, with a few small tweaks, can see you reaching 60mph in around six seconds. After quite a few more tweaks, the later 'bomb proof' four-cylinder Red Block engines can cope with upwards of 600bhp, and will happily shame near enough anything on the road.

Flat ground is the best place to be in a rear-wheel drive Volvo when it's snowing.

While not ideal for handling, a relatively high ground clearance means you're not likely to scrape the car anywhere on the road. This combined with heavy engineering and a high build quality means you can be confident on rough ground and verges too. However, despite the many benefits of rear-wheel drive, don't expect to be climbing any hills if snow becomes compacted and slippery. Whilst first gear is a low ratio, the engines produce a lot of torque and there's comparatively little weight over the driven wheels at the rear, meaning you could be caught out on occasion.

4 Relative values
– which model for you?

With a wide variety of engines, options, and most crucially, uses, selling prices are mainly sensitive to condition above all else. There are some trends however. Diesel models tend to be available for slightly less, and the 2.3-litre turbo models are becoming very rare and generally fetch more. Most notable of all are the 780 models, of which only around 8500 were made. This rarity

Extensive luxury, but limos can be difficult to sell on.

can command high prices but they're not as appealing to some, having only been produced as left-hand drive models.

Due to the variances in condition, the information below should be used as a guide only, and supplemented by the further detail on value in chapters to follow, as well as local price guides. The list starts with the highest priced model at 100 per cent with the remainder shown as a percentage of that value.

780 Turbo 16V 2.0-litre . . . . .100 per cent
780 Turbo 2.5-litre. . . . . 89 per cent
780 V6 2.8-litre . . . . 83 per cent
780 Turbo Diesel 2.4-litre . . . . 78 per cent
740 Turbo Intercooler 2.3-litre.. . . . . 28 per cent
740 GLT 16V 2.3-litre . . . . 26 per cent
S90 24v 2.9-litre. . . . . 26 per cent
960 24v 2.9-litre . . . . 22 per cent
960 Turbo Intercooler 2.3-litre.. . . . . 18 per cent
940 SE 2.0-litre .. . . 15 per cent
740 Turbo Diesel 2.4-litre . . . . 13 per cent
740 GL 2.3-litre .. . . 13 per cent

Even workhorses can be in good condition.

5 Before you view
– be well informed

Going to view the car you end up buying can be a great experience, so be clear about the answers you want to hear before you hand over your cash. In addition to the considerations below, making a list of the questions most important to you and getting them answered with a short email or call to the seller, can often save you the disappointment of a wasted journey.

Don't forget to check the current values of the models you are interested in, using car magazines that feature price guides. Online sale listings and auction sites can also be a great way to get a feel for how general condition and model specific extras can affect prices.

Where is the car?

Is it going to be worth travelling some distance to view the car? Having received an email response or talked with the seller by phone, you'll be better able to judge their appreciation of the journey you'll have to make, and how accommodating

It's worth viewing cars close to home; even if not exactly what you are looking for, it might widen your horizons.

they're likely to be for your assessments when you arrive.

Models closer to home may not be exactly what you're looking for, but the little effort involved will provide you with invaluable experience for the more important candidate to come. You may even be surprised by what you find locally.

Dealer or private sale?

Establish early on if a car is being sold by its owner or by a trader. A private owner should have all the history. A dealer may have more limited knowledge of a car's history, but should have some documentation. A dealer may offer a warranty/guarantee (ask for a printed copy), and finance.

Cost of collection and delivery?

A dealer may well be used to quoting for delivery by car transporter. A private owner may agree to meet you halfway, but only agree to this after you have seen the car at the vendor's address to validate the documents. You could meet halfway and agree the sale, but insist on meeting at the vendor's address for the handover.

View: when and where?

It is always preferable to view at the vendor's home or business premises. In the case of a private sale, the car's documentation should tally with the vendor's name and address. Arrange to view only in daylight and avoid a wet day: most cars look better in poor light or when wet.

Reason for sale?
Do make it one of the first questions you ask. Why is the car being sold, and how long has it been with the current owner? How many previous owners have there been?

Conversions & modifications?
Modified examples, or those with replacement or different engines fitted must be given further attention to determine the reason for the changes, the suitability and compatibility of non-original parts, and the competency of those that undertook the work.

Condition?
Ask for an honest appraisal of the car's condition. Ask specifically about some of the check items described in chapter 7.

All original specification?
An original equipment car is normally of higher value than a customized version. However some modifications can add value due to the benefits and rarity

This rather rare 740 estate has seen better days.

of the parts involved. For example, if an M90 gearbox has been fitted to a 740 to modernize the gear shifting and do away with the overdrive, this can add value due to the quality and rarity of the gearbox. As always, be sure of the age and condition of any parts changed as well as seeking conformation of a proficient fitment, such as a receipt from a reputable mechanic.

Derrick's tasteful modifications are not likely to adversely affect value.

Matching data/legal ownership?

Do the VIN/chassis, engine numbers and licence plate match the official registration documents? For those countries that require an annual test of roadworthiness, does the car have a document showing that it complies? (an MOT certificate in the UK, which can be verified on 0845 600 5977)

If a smog/emissions certificate is mandatory, does the car have one? If required, does the car carry a current road fund licence plate tag?

Does the vendor own the car outright? Money might be owed to a finance company or bank; the car could even be stolen. For a fee, several organizations will supply the ownership data, based on the car's licence plate number. Such companies can often also tell you if a car has been 'written-off' by an insurance company. The following organizations can supply data:

```
HPI  .. .. .. .. .. .. .. .. .. .. .. .. .. .. .. .. .. .. .. .01722 422 422 (UK)
AA . .. .. .. .. .. .. .. .. .. .. .. .. .. .. .. .. .. .. .. .0870 600 0836 (UK)
DVLA . .. .. .. .. .. .. .. .. .. .. .. .. .. .. .. .. .. .. .0870 240 0010 (UK)
RAC .. .. .. .. .. .. .. .. .. .. .. .. .. .. .. .. .. .. .. .0870 533 3660 (UK)
Carfax  .. .. .. .. .. .. .. .. .. .. .. .. .. .. .. .. http://www.carfax.com (USA)
Autocheck . .. .. .. .. .. .. .. .. .. .. .. .. .. .http://www.autocheck.com (USA)
```

Other countries will have similar organizations.

Insurance?

Check with your existing insurer before setting out, as your current policy might not cover you to drive the car if you do purchase it.

How you can pay

A cheque will take several days to clear and the seller may prefer to sell to a cash buyer. However, a bankers draft (a cheque issued by a bank) is as good as cash but safer, so contact your own bank and become familiar with formalities that are necessary to obtain one.

Buying at auction

If the intention is to buy at auction, see chapter 10 for further advice.

Professional vehicle check (mechanical examination)

There are often marque/model specialists who will undertake professional examination of a vehicle on your behalf. Owners' clubs will be able to put you in touch with such specialists. Other organizations that will carry out a general professional check include:

```
AA . .. .. .. .. .. 0800 085 3007 (UK motoring organization with vehicle inspectors)
ABS .. .. .. .. .. .. .. .. 0800 358 5855 (UK specialist vehicle inspection company)
RAC .. .. .. .. .. 0870 533 3660 (UK motoring organization with vehicle inspectors)
AAA .. .. .. http://www.aaa.com (USA motoring organization with vehicle inspection
                                                                        centres)
```

Other countries will have similar organizations.

6 Inspection equipment
– these items will really help

Before you rush out of the door, gather together a few items that will help as you work your way around the car.

Don't forget to take the essentials with you when viewing a car.

This book
This book is designed to be your guide at every step, so take it along with you and use the check boxes to help you assess each area of the car you're interested in. Don't be afraid to let the seller see you using it.

Glasses (spectacles)
Take your reading glasses if you need them to read documents and make close up inspections.

Magnet (not powerful, a fridge magnet is ideal)
A magnet will help you check if the car is full of filler or has fibreglass panels. Use the magnet to sample bodywork areas around the car, but be careful not to damage the paintwork. Expect to find a little filler here and there, but not whole panels. There's nothing wrong with fibreglass panels, but a purist might want the car to be as original as possible.

Torch
A torch with fresh batteries will be useful for peering into the wheel arches and under the car.

Seals and join areas are most vulnerable to rust.
(Courtesy Dustin Hulting)

Probe or small screwdriver

A small screwdriver can be used – with care – as a probe, particularly in the wheel arches and on the underside. With this you should be able to check any area of severe corrosion, but be careful – if it's really bad the screwdriver may go through the metal!

Overalls

Be prepared to get dirty. Take along a pair of overalls if you have them, or use some clothes you'd be prepared to throw away.

Mirror on a stick

Fixing a mirror at an angle on the end of a stick may seem odd, but you'll probably need it to check the condition of the underside of the car thoroughly. It will also help you to peer into some of the important crevices. You can also use it, together with the torch, along the underside of the sill and on the floor.

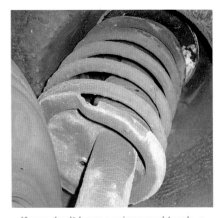

If you don't have a mirror and torch, a decent camera phone with flash can help you see where your head won't fit!

Digital camera

If you have the use of a digital camera, take it along so you can study some areas of the car more closely at your leisure. Take a picture of any part of the car that causes you concern, and seek a knowledgeable friend's opinion. Ideally, have a friend or knowledgeable enthusiast accompany you: a second opinion is always valuable.

The brown ring around this light lens is a clear sign that the seal has failed.

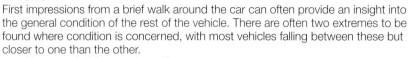

Exterior

First impressions from a brief walk around the car can often provide an insight into the general condition of the rest of the vehicle. There are often two extremes to be found where condition is concerned, with most vehicles falling between these but closer to one than the other.

At one end of the spectrum there are a number of examples that have been very well maintained, and in some cases appear immaculate. Rear-wheel drive Volvos are in a niche part of the market and for those that appreciate the advantages, it's not uncommon to find many years of ownership with well documented maintenance and care.

The above average length of ownership is one of the reasons that general appearance will often be consistent with overall condition, and means you are unlikely to find gleaming examples that are falling apart beneath the surface.

Something to aspire to, perhaps.

At the other end of the spectrum there are examples that have clearly had a tough working life. If cosmetic appearance is not so high on your list of priorities, however, then scratches, dents and wear aren't necessarily reason alone to dismiss the candidate, as these Volvos can take a great deal of physical abuse, provided they are also regularly maintained in the essential areas.

Begin by examining the stance of the car to check for wear or damage to the suspension. For example, an estate with a sagging rear end is most likely to have done a lot of load carrying, and may need new springs to restore ride quality.

Check the fit and alignment of body panels, lights, doors, the boot/tail gate, the bonnet/hood, bumpers and trim. The congruency cannot compete with the modern precision found on a Lexus, for example, but was superior enough in its day, and mismatched lines will give you a cue to investigate further should you find any.

You're unlikely to find rust on the bodywork, and you'll only usually find some surface rust on the exposed area of a dent or chip if it has been there for around a year. Trim around windows and paint around the bottom corners and edges of the front and rear screens can begin to bubble and peel a little. This is to be expected on older examples, but any excessive deterioration – including to the rubber seals in these areas – will need work in future.

Underbody

With generous ground clearance (as cars go), there should be enough space to perform a quick check of the

This window seal is not doing its job at one end.

underside without the need for lifting equipment. A quick check around the wheelarches and sills with an angled mirror is faster than trying to move your head around each wheel. However, when under the car do have a closer look at the support structure behind the wheels, where use over less than ideal road surfaces would cause the most wear and damage, if any. Volvo provided a generous amount of undercoating, especially on earlier models; however the amount and quality of application has been known to vary, so check for what should be a thick and even coat in order to reassure yourself.

If you can reach, check for any play with a firm shake of the prop shaft, panhard rod, anti-roll bars, steering gear and suspension control rods. Finally, check for any fluid leaks, particularly around the differential.

A dry differential exterior is a good sign, but there appears to be a leak from the spare wheel well.

Most four-cylinder ID strips are on the belt cover ...

Interior
Interiors are generally tough compared to most standards, and while not as warm and inviting as some, the strong lines surrounding those comfortable seats will make you feel as safe as Volvos are famed for.

The main let-down is the plastics, which can be prone to cracking in hotter climes, with the textured plastic found around the rear view mirror, for example, becoming brittle with age. Also check the arm rest: the rear passenger ash tray draw mechanism, and the closure stud on the lid of the arm rest pocket are prone to breaking.

... although there is usually an information plate on the block.

While inside, also check the electrical functions are working, together with the seat belts; not forgetting the seat adjustments if they're manually-operated.

Engines
A wide range of engines were fitted to the 700/900 Series Volvos. There are three variants of Volkswagen's straight-six diesel engine: the D24 (normally-aspirated), D24T (turbo), and D24Tic (turbo intercooler).

The relevant petrol engine codes all begin with a letter 'B' for bensin, which means 'gasoline' in Swedish. The numbers that follow denote the engine size, the number of valves-per-cylinder (the last digit), and after 1993, the number of cylinders (as the first digit where used):

Code	Series	Configuration	Size	Valve arrangement
B23	700	4cyl	2.3l	8v
B200	All	4cyl	2.0l	8v
B204	All	4cyl	2.0l	16v
B230	All	4cyl	2.3l	8v
B234	All	4cyl	2.3l	16v
B280	All	V6	2.8l	12v
B6244	960/S90/V90	6cyl	2.4l	24v
B6254	960/S90/V90	6cyl	2.5l	24v
B6304	960/S90/V90	6cyl	2.9l	24v

A run-through of the key points to check with each type of engine is covered in chapter 8, and further details of engine identification follow in the next section.

Paperwork/ownership/legality

Checking the documentation that's offered with the sale is crucial. If there is official service history, it's always a good sign of methodical maintenance, and while not essential, full service history is very reassuring, especially when considering that 700/900s can fetch a good price even with high mileage attached. It's the regular maintenance that makes the difference between a Volvo that will eat your wallet and one that will sail toward achieving 300,000 miles.

Seeing when servicing tasks were last completed will also serve to guide you as to what will need completing next, and how soon you should think about spending a little to keep things running well.

If you're still interested after all your checks, take a look at the vehicle registration certificate (form V5C in the UK). Ensure that the information there tallies with the identification plates on the vehicle and statistical information in chapter 17. The vehicle identification plate is located on the inner-most left-hand corner of the engine bay when standing in front of the car. The engine identification is located on the front-face of the belt assembly cover on most four-cylinder engines, the right-hand side of the cylinder head for diesel models, and the back-left corner at the top of V6 engines.

If you are examining the car at an address other than that on the registration certificate, you should be satisfied as to why.

Final thought checklist

Is the condition of the body and paintwork what you expected?

Are you sure that any faults you have found can be repaired, or do you need further advice?

Are the main structural and mechanical areas in good condition, lessening the risk of any big surprises?

If you have found problems or work you feel needs to be done, has this been reflected in the sale price?

Imagine the reality of owning the vehicle, and don't let your heart rule your head.

Volvos are great at towing but eventually the springs will sag – best keep this yacht on the water!

8 Key points
– where to look for problems

General engine points

Remove the oil filler cap to check for a sludge-like residue. This is indicative of a serious problem, most commonly a head gasket failure.

Check the colour of the oil to see if it needs changing, and compare this to when the seller says it was last done.

Looking through the oil fill opening, check for tarnishing on the lobes of the camshaft. This is an indication that oil changes have been neglected.

A low oil level could be a sign that the car is leaking or burning oil.

This mess is likely to have overflowed via the filler cap.

700 Series models with carburettors should idle at around 900rpm. If idling too high, the carburettor could be poorly adjusted or the vacuum may be stuck or damaged. Carburettors are generally trouble free, but parts can be very hard to find for some Pierburg models so they should be checked thoroughly.

Black smoke from the exhaust is an indication that the fuel mixture is too rich. This could be an automatic choke (as fitted to some Pierburg models) stuck in position, a blocked air filter, faulty fuel pressure regulator or broken engine sensor.

Blue smoke means that oil is burning. If this occurs for a short time before disappearing, it's likely to be worn valve guides or seals. However, continual blue smoke is a bad sign, often caused by a badly worn turbo (if fitted) or piston rings.

A small amount of white smoke is excusable on a cold, damp day when there is a lot of moisture in the air. However, white smoke on a drier day, or an excessive amount, is indicative of water entering the combustion system. This is usually caused by a blown head gasket, but could also be due to a broken head or cylinder wall. From an automatic, white smoke can also be caused by a faulty gearbox modulator allowing transmission fluid into the system.

Red block engines

The 2-litre and 2.3-litre petrol/gas engines used by the majority of 700/900 Series Volvos are so named after their distinctive red paint. They are widely regarded

This is how an engine bay should look!

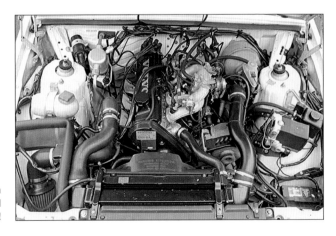

as some of the strongest and most reliable engines around, playing a central role in these cars' reputation for durability.

Minor high-pitched rustling coming from the engine and a muted tappet noise coming from the rocker cover at idle are normal for these engines, although should disappear as you rev away from idle.

Regardless of the above, regular oil changes are as essential as they are with any engine for keeping things on track toward the huge number of miles that these units can rack up. This is especially important for the health of the turbo if fitted, therefore well documented service history reflecting this is welcomed.

A little loss of oil is acceptable, but check with the seller that consumption is not excessive.

Later models were fitted with up rated oil distribution channels in the block.

Diesel engines

Whilst not as quiet as modern diesels, the 2.4-litre six-cylinder Volkswagen diesel engines used in 700/900 Series cars were very smooth, comfortable units to drive with for their day.

They rival the Red Block for reliability but generally require more regular servicing, so a good service history is advised.

All units are an interference valve arrangement, so make sure the timing belt has been changed recently enough.

Check for cracks around the head and top of the block.

It's very easy to spot good and bad examples at either end of the scale

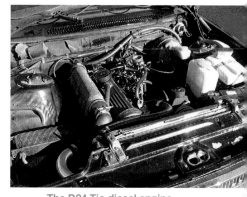

The D24 Tic diesel engine.

using two simple measures. Starting quickly and strongly from cold and holding idle without too much help is a good sign. If the engine takes a while this could simply be worn glow plugs, which are cheap enough to fix. However, this could also mean low compression caused by a worn engine.

Secondly, thick and continual smoke of any colour coming from the exhaust is another indication of wear and if combined with a difficult start you may be better off walking away.

On turbo models there should be a distinctive tractor-like whistle coming from the turbo as it spools up. If this is not the case the turbo is not making pressure.

V6 engines

The V6 units are the most sensitive to service requirements of all the engines in the range, so a full service history is essential as they can be very costly to repair. Well-serviced V6 engines with religious oil changes can be very reliable.

The older B28 variant found on some 700 Series cars has narrow oil channels that can become blocked causing rapid wear to the engine area affected by the lack of lubrication.

Take extra care when checking for oil and water leaks as these can be expensive to rectify on V6 engines.

The camshafts are controlled by a timing chain which is generally trouble free but check closely for any unusual noises indicating wear.

It's normal for these engines to sound a little like a diesel van, but they should rev smoothly with very little vibration.

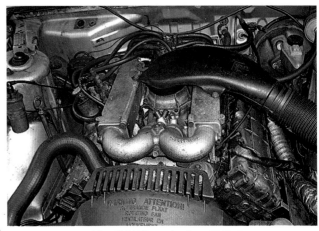

The PRV V6 engine in a GLE.

24V engines

The 2.9-litre and later 2.5-litre 24 valve straight-six engines gave birth to Volvo's modular engine range and can be found on S90, V90 and late 960 models. With these cars being the basis for development of the 850, their six-cylinder engines are virtually the same as the five-cylinder offspring that was used.

Whilst not as indestructible as a Red Block, the engines themselves are very reliable with the only real weak point being the timing belt. To begin with these were not very strong, and the various pulleys and tensioners had to be kept in good order, with regular changes of the timing belt. This provides piece of mind, as the valve assembly is an interference fit.

This situation improved year-on-

The later 24v Straight 6 modular engine fills the engine bay well.

year with the strongest version appearing in 1995. Check when the timing belt was last changed regardless. Like the V6 engines, the straight-sixes are very smooth and shouldn't vibrate excessively. Should you hear a tappet noise from the rocker cover, it is likely resultant from wear to the valves and camshaft assembly.

9 Serious evaluation
– 60 minutes for years of enjoyment

Score each section as follows: 4 = excellent; 3 = good; 2 = average; 1 = poor. The totting up procedure is detailed at the end of the chapter. Try to remain consistent and realistic in scoring each section.

It's understandable that keeping a seller waiting while you examine the car thoroughly is uncomfortable for most people, but you must not be rushed if you're to have no regrets once the car has been bought. Most sellers respond well to an enthusiastic approach, together with the odd bit of praise for the well kept parts of the car. Of course, if there are no well kept parts of the car, you may have dismissed the venture after the 15 minute evaluation.

Talking with the seller while completing your checks can be distracting, but using the following checklist and being sure to record your scores and comments for later will ensure you don't forget anything.

Exterior
Volvo 700/900 exteriors are normally a good rough indicator of the car's general condition. Common sense dictates that if a car appears to be in a generally tired and shabby state, it's likely to have been treated as such. This may well be reflected in the parts of the car you can't see. Likewise, if a car appears well kept, it often is. While this initial judgement is rarely truer than with Volvos of this era, it's still useful and reassuring to delve deeper and confirm, as it is with any other vehicle.

For example, if cosmetic appearance is not as important to you and you're just looking for a sound mechanical example, an evaluation using the scoring system that follows could unearth the car you're looking for – a poor outward condition will put other buyers off. If you find the rest of the car to be in an acceptable working condition you could be in for a bargain.

Conversely, a thorough check could

This 940 seems in good order from the outside, but it's always worth delving deeper.

reveal an outwardly gleaming example to possess a fault that even the owner may not have been aware of. This will give you better insight into what needs doing once you own the car, and will give you some bargaining power when you come to discuss the price.

Paintwork

The paintwork on these cars generally lasts very well if it's been looked after, and it wouldn't be too unreasonable to expect a well maintained example to have almost new looking paintwork.

Check that the paintwork is even in colour and tone across the whole car. If there are variations in thickness, or colour differences in one particular area, there may have been repair work. Check with the seller to get their side of the story. If in doubt, check the paint code which is located on the VIN plate in the engine bay, and ensure that this matches the vehicle's registration document. If not, there needs to be a good reason. Another way to ascertain if there has been a respray is to check for a previous paint colour in hard-to-reach areas.

Bodywork   4   3   2   1

Volvo used thick, well-protected metal on most of the bodywork, but this was not galvanized as standard until 1987, so examples prior to this may suffer from rust.

Once introduced, the galvanizing was very effective, and even if you find dents which expose the metal bodywork, you're unlikely to find rust so long as the dent is away from the edges of panels, or join areas where water can collect. If such a dent is showing signs of rust it's likely to have gone untreated for a long time or may have spent its life near the sea, where salt accelerates rust. Other areas where water could collect, including joint areas within the engine bay, are further places to check to ensure they are sound. It's not unusual to find surface rust in the gutter of the roof rails, but even this is unlikely to be anything severe.

The inside of window frames, the battery tray, chassis beams and joins to the subframe are all rust-prone areas to check. Aluminium tailgates on estates are prone to corrosion and paint disruption.

Excellent drainage hoses but when blocked can cause rust as has taken hold next to the boot seal.

Stone chips are likely to be found on any vehicle of a certain age, but there's often more noticeable damage to coloured plastic trim. Check these areas around the front of the car, and don't forget the areas of bodywork behind the wheels, which could suffer from debris kicked up by the tyres.

Join areas   4   3   2   1

The framework and rubber trim around windows don't always match up to the tough standards set by the majority of the car. Years of cold temperatures and/or hot sunlight can cause rubber seals to bend upward. If you can't see any bending also check that the area is clean and firmly pressed onto the glass. Algae and moss left to grow around windows can force itself between seals and glass, causing permanent deformation.

The areas where body panels meet should be even and level. The simple body lines of 700/900 Series Volvos make it easy to spot bad alignment. Any excessive misalignments may require further investigation: for example, uneven shut lines on doors might be caused by one or two worn hinges.

Wheelarches   4   3   2   1

If you are concerned about rust on any car, in and around the wheelarches is where you are most likely to find it. Excessive amounts of mud build-up or debris damage could be a sign of regular misuse off-road. The rear arches are likely to be worse affected where wheel spinning has directed more debris their way.

Trim & bumpers   4   3   2   1

Bumpers on 700 Series models stand proud of the car and are very tough. They

Scratches are well disguised on the older, unpainted bumpers.

The plastic on this wing mirror has faded somewhat in the sun.

can take many knocks and scrapes with their collapsible sides, which only show on closer inspection as they are unpainted. Both 700 and 900 Series models have front and rear gas filled buffers inside the bumpers, which cushion small impact forces from accidental bumps through the chassis. This avoids damage to other areas of the car including to the bumper itself. Later S90 and V90 models adopted the more modern painted bumpers that sweep around the car in one unit. Damage to these is both more noticeable and often more costly.

Glass

As well as overall condition, check to ensure that the windows slide smoothly into the tops of the door frames. Any difficulties here may be an indication of a damaged, misaligned or broken window mechanism.

Also check that any identification numbers etched onto the windows (normally the VIN number in the UK) match those stamped elsewhere on the car and on the official ownership documents. It's not a good sign if this etching appears to have been intentionally scratched or distorted. If glass has been replaced it may be an indication of the car having been in an accident. Without a satisfactory explanation this would warrant further investigation.

Wipers

Due to their short height and steep angle, saloon (sedan) rear windscreens were not fitted with wipers, however heat wires and cabin blower ducting serve to fend off condensation or snow. A single rear wiper and washer was fitted to estate models. Miniature headlamp wipers and washers were fitted to all models.

Wiper rubber should be clean, flexible and maintain a good even pressure on the surface of the glass. Also check to ensure movement is smooth and that there is no juddering.

Wheels

Volvo made a large variety of wheels for the 700/900 Series cars, including both steel and alloys. Check alloys for kerbing marks, and cracks or buckling. Steel wheels only normally deform at the edge with lighter impacts but this could stop hub caps seating properly. Check under hubcaps too if concerned. Be aware that while there are a lot of secondhand wheels out there, replacing wheels with an exact match may not be an option.

If the wheels are very poor and you're considering aftermarket wheels, remember that all models, save for the very late 960's (which share an offset of ET42 with later front-wheel drive models), have a very small offset of ET25. This combined with the unusual stud pattern of 5x108 PCD (pitch circle diameter) means you're likely to need wheel spacers if you want much of a choice in wheel style.

Volvo Draco wheels as fitted to early turbos are becoming rare.

Tyres

In the UK, tyres must be the same size and construction type on opposing sides. However, it is permissible to have different sizes for front and rear. Wider tyres at the rear of these big cars do look good, but the performance is more reliant on tyres being a good match with the wheels they're fitted to.

Tyre tread depth must be at least 1.6mm across 75 per cent of the width of the tyre. Any cuts greater than 25mm or 10 per cent of the width tyre, that expose the ply or cords, render the tyre illegal. The same goes for any abrasion or wear that exposes the tyre ply, or bulges caused by structural failure. Also ensure the tyres are all sufficiently inflated.

Quite apart from the risk of a tyre being illegal, any excessive or uneven wear is a likely indicator to other problems with the car. It could simply be a matter of uneven tyre pressures, but may equally be caused by incorrect wheel alignment, worn hub bearings, worn bushes or even a bent chassis or bent suspension components. If you're still in any doubt after exhausting the investigations detailed in this book, take the advice of an experienced friend as a second opinion.

Tyre depth should satisfy the legal limits across at least 75 per cent of the width of the tyre.

Mechanical components

Checking the core working components of the car is often the most unappealing task. You're likely to have to reach around a bit and get dirty but these checks are important.

General engine bay

The large flat bonnet (hood) sported by 700/900 Series Volvos unsurprisingly has a lot of room underneath. This is well filled by the V6 engines, where a number of key ancillaries are located on the opposite side to the in-line four-cylinder engines. For example, the dipstick is

The vertical lift position is very useful for working deep in the engine bay or when removing engines.

located on the left ahead of the brake reservoir, unlike the

Testing the lock on the scissor mechanism of the bonnet (hood) hinges.

four-cylinder engines where it is located on the right, behind the inlet manifold. When opening the bonnet, check that the hinges are in good condition, the springs comfortably hold the bonnet open and the latches on the scissor mechanism operate as they should, allowing you to further open the bonnet to a vertical position.

Identification numbers

The main VIN (vehicle identification number) plate can be found under the bonnet, normally on the chassis, either rearward of the left suspension mount or rearward of the left headlight. Check the information on it as described in chapter 11. The body number is located on the chassis rearward of the right headlight.

The location of engine identification numbers is described in chapter 7.

The VIN plate mounted here behind the offside head lamp.

The body number shown here behind the nearside headlight.

Battery

All turbo models (including diesels) have the battery on the right hand side, with other engines locating it on the opposite side. Battery terminals form a light layer of corrosion on them over time. This will give a very rough indication of age, so check with the owner when the battery was last replaced.

Fuse box & ECU

The fuse box is located behind the ash tray in the centre console, and, together with the main relays behind it, forms the central electrical unit. Access the fuse box by pressing the lever at the base of the ash tray to remove it completely. Individual fuses can be tested using a testing light. The centre console would have to be removed to check and replace any relays following relevant electrical failure, but it will rarely be necessary to do so.

You can change a fuse while sitting in the driver's seat.

Airbox & induction

The airbox is located at the front of the car and depending on the engine, will be located either on the left or the right hand side. Filters are relatively inexpensive to replace but failure to do so for a long period of time can cause premature engine

Cone filters can provide better performance.

wear. Knock on the airbox. If there is an excessive amount of dust in the area, it's likely the filter is way overdue a change. Check the paperwork with the car to see when it was last changed and, if necessary, ask if you can open the airbox and have a look.

Fuel-injection system/carburettor
A variety of Bosch systems were fitted to these cars starting with the basic Motronic injection system and developing from there. Generally, faults with fuel-injection manifest themselves at idle or on acceleration, as the ECU will make minor adjustments where needed. However, an improperly adjusted carburettor can fuel an engine with little outward effect, whilst causing premature wear. Aside from a poor idle, a good indication of a poorly adjusted carburettor is the condition of the sparkplugs.

Sparkplugs
Inspecting the sparkplugs means removing them, so if this is required, come prepared with a sparkplug removal socket and wrench. After removing the HT leads, check the condition of the terminal's contact area for corrosion. Once the sparkplug has been removed, check the overall condition of the firing end. Excessive black sooty deposits could be a sign of an over-rich fuel mixture. Conversely, dark, heavily glazed electrodes could be a sign of an over-lean mixture. More detailed guides can be easily found online or in any ownership manual.

Wiring & ignition system
Engine bay wiring has to face some harsh conditions throughout its life. The continual cycle of heat from a running engine followed by cooling between journeys can cause wiring insulation to harden and even crack over time. This wear can accelerate in colder areas. HT leads produce a significant amount of heat of their own. It may be worth investing in silicone leads if you live in harsher climes.

Warmer areas can cause problems with dust, and no matter where you are, moisture and electrical components don't mix well, especially nearer the sea. Check the condition of the insulation around any wiring in the engine bay you can find, especially the HT leads. Don't forget to examine any exposed or suspicious looking connections as well.

Hoses & cooling system
Use a torch to gain a better view of the radiator through the front grille, and ensure that the majority of the tiny fins are straight and undamaged. The efficiency of a radiator can be increased immensely by simply giving it a thorough clean to improve the flow between these fins, so the less debris you find the better. It's worth performing the same check to the engine side of the radiator, as damage could have been caused by someone working on the vehicle. If viewing a turbo model,

Check the fins of all cooling units, including the oil radiator where fitted.

inspect the intercooler in the same manor.

Not all leaks from cooling systems are evident immediately. Leaks may only occur under the increased pressure of a warm running engine. Check the underside of metal hose clamps and bodywork immediately below radiator hose unions. Localised rust in one patch may be an indication of a leak.

This hose clamp has seen better days, but should be at no risk of breaking.

As with wiring, rubber hoses that have lost all pliability have an increased chance of cracking and should be considered for replacement. Also check for cracks around clamping areas caused by excessive pinching. Finally check that the radiator's fan is in good working order, the last place you want your engine to overheat is in static traffic where it's needed most.

Belts

Exposed and accessible belts can be examined for cracks and checked for tension; a firm thumb press should deflect the belt no more than 10-15mm at the middle of the longest run. The timing belt will be behind a cover and the documented history should be checked for the last time this was changed. If this was over 80,000 miles ago, it's overdue. Also check for when other belts were changed, regardless of inspection.

The Red Block timing belt is snugly located behind the other belts with its cover.

Gaskets & manifolds

Check around the inlet and exhaust manifolds to evaluate the condition of the gaskets. Ensure the heat shielding around the exhaust area is not rusting and is securely attached. The rest of the exhaust, including the downpipe, can be checked when looking under the car later. Look for any leaks around the rocker cover gasket. This is often not changed as regularly as it should be. Oil on just the top area of the cover near the filler, may simply be spillage, or the requirement of a new filler cap seal.

Some surface rust on the heat shields, but be more concerned about the amount of oil getting down there.

Turbocharger (where fitted)

If you have the opportunity, remove the intake hose for a quick inspection of the turbine. Try to move it side to side and up and down within its housing. Play in any direction should be barely perceptible. Petrol turbo units with small cracks in the exhaust housing have been known to run without noticeable ill-effect but if spotted, this is never ideal and may get worse.

Further signs of the turbo's condition will be evident later by noise, performance and possibly by smoke emitted by the exhaust.

Stress-free checks
Many of the checks that follow can be done with the car on the ground if you cannot raise the car for whatever reason. However, things will be much easier and more thorough if you can raise the car up using a jack, or better still a ramp that takes the load off the wheels (placing the car in a stress free condition).

Engine mounts

Even the smallest 2.0 litre engines are torquey units. This combined with being longitudinally mounted means the engine could move about a lot when revved. To accommodate this Volvo have cradled engines using a sturdy brace for mounting as well as other braces for the gearbox, etc. Check that these are in good condition, paying particular attention to the rubber components, ensuring they are not cracked or loose.

Exhaust system
The older single curve tail pipes tend to be the most susceptible to rust, however, this is normally just a cosmetic issue. If more urgent problems exist, they are likely to be found at the welded seams or pipe unions of cans and mufflers, where water can collect and cause rust. Pay these areas special attention when performing a general check for rust. Also check the downpipes of diesel and V6 engines carefully as replacements are now hard to find.

Any amount of moisture in the air also means this passes through the inside of the exhaust after being expelled by the engine. As a result, some exhaust cans and mufflers can appear fine on outward inspection, with rust taking hold internally. One way to test for this without removal is to tap the muffler and listen for any rattles or shaking of rusting debris.

Next, check for any areas where the exhaust system may be rubbing or banging against other parts of the car. This will either be due to incorrectly sized replacement parts, a poorly mounted exhaust, or worn and sagging mounting rubbers, so check these areas too.

Finally, when it comes to switching the engine on, check the exhaust for any leaks, especially around joints. Have someone momentarily cover the end of the exhaust with a rag, as this will accentuate any leaking hisses or blows further up the pipe work.

Suspension shocks & pivots
In most models that use a live rear axle, the panhard rod is basically all that keeps the rear wheels laterally aligned with the body. Misalignment of the rear wheels may indicate a bent panhard rod mount, which could be costly to fix.

Check there is no excessive play in

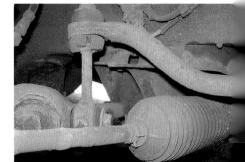

This bushing needs replacing as soon as possible.

the suspension pivots both front and rear and ensure the rubber bushes are sound. The most usual to fail are those on the lower rear trailing arms.

Steering gear

The steering gear has similar articulated joints to suspension articulations. They should be checked in the same way but bearing in mind that steering failure can be far more catastrophic. Pay particular attention to the ball joints and their seals. If the vehicle is in a stress-free condition, grasp a front wheel and move back and forth as if steering the wheel by hand. While doing so, feel for any play in the steering joints. Further feedback from the steering may be noted when test driving the car later. Check the power steering fluid level is within parameters and is a clear red colour. Dark murky fluid should be replaced.

This control arm has been polished by tyres that are too wide.

Wheel bearings

Grasping the wheel with hands now at the six o'clock position (so as not to induce steering), apply the same rocking motion as above. Notable play in this case is likely to be caused by a worn wheel bearing. The wheel should rotate freely and easily. Don't forget to check the rear wheels as well. Worn wheel bearings may also be detected by a squealing or grinding noise when driving.

Brakes

The brakes are generally strong, and they need to be for a car of this size and weight. When inspecting, ensure that there is plenty of pad thickness left and that the disc surfaces are smooth and shiny. If there is a lip on the outer edge of the disc surface that is easily spotted with the naked eye, the discs should be considered for replacement. A light surface film of rust is normal if the car has not been driven for a few days, but should easily clean off under braking when test driving the car. Check the colour of the brake fluid and the level: it should be a light golden colour and topped up to within the markings. Dark-coloured brake fluid indicates that it's old and could do with replacing.

Clutch

Both 700 and 900 Series cars were available with either a cable-operated or hydraulic clutch depending on the year and market. Generally, non-turbo cars before 1990 were fitted with cable clutches that require periodic wear adjustment throughout their life. If experiencing a high biting point from a cable clutch, check that it is adjusted properly before assuming a replacement is required.

Hydraulic clutches self-adjust, and there should be no need to use the adjustable nut as fitted to the slave rods on some models. Bear in mind that a high biting point is normal in these cars. The clutches last well and once slipping is detected when driving, gentle application of the throttle should ensure the clutch remains useable until a garage appointment can be made.

Gearbox

A variety of transmissions were fitted to 700/900 Series cars. Automatic gearboxes were either Toyota's A class transmission or ZF Friedrichshafen four-speed boxes. Both were solid units but vulnerable if excessively revved in park or neutral, which can burn out the torque converter.

The M90 gearbox (foreground) next to an older M46.

700 Series and earlier 900 Series manual cars were fitted with an M46 (four-speed plus overdrive) or less commonly, M47 (five-speed) gearbox. It's normal for these to sound rather clunky and industrial when shifting between first and reverse. However, noise when on the move is not a good sign; check the transmission oil for evidence of metal particles, as this could be expensive to put right.

The strongest manual variant is the M90 box found in 900 Series cars from 1995 onward. These are a lot smoother and brought the driving experience more up to date. Even so, too many missed shifts into third gear could cause premature failure until a revised version rectified the problem in 1997.

Prop shaft & differential

4 3 2 1

For the propeller shaft, check all the flange bolts are tight and in sound condition. Check the universal joint and central bearing for play or wear. Finally ensure the rubber coupling is in good condition and not misshapen or cracked.

There are three different types of differential found on these cars. Regardless of it being a standard open differential, clutch operated limited slip, or a mechanically locking differential, it will need to be checked around the casing for any signs of oil leaks, as matching replacements are hard to find, and a professional overhaul can be costly. Also check that there is no play and a good seal at the input shaft and the two half shafts.

Undercoating

4 3 2 1

The undercoating on most models was applied thickly and evenly, however, variations occur. Check for any areas affected by stones or debris and note any missed areas to keep an eye on in the future as these may be more susceptible to damage or rust.

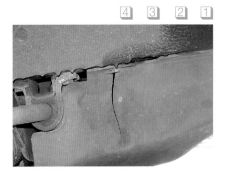

An area to keep an eye on. Flying debris could result in this cracked undertray hanging off.

Interior

Checking the interior of your prospective purchase can often be a rushed job. You've done the hard part and sometimes people just sit in the drives seat, and limit their view to what can be see in this comfortable position. Of course, getting a feel for daily life with the car is important, but there's plenty of time for sitting down when test driving!

Boot (trunk)

Check the condition of the carpet. Any stains are a sign that water may have pooled here as a result of a leak. Lift up the carpet to check for rust, paying special attention to the base of the rear and side walls, the spare wheel well and the wells or storage areas in the rear quarters. It's also worth noting the condition of any drainage bungs fitted. If any are missing, this could lead to ingress of water coming up from under the car.

Also check the boot seal: clean and tight is the key to keeping your valuables dry.

Spare wheel & jack

The spare wheel can tell you a fair amount about the owner and their level of care. A matching or well chosen weight saving spare, in good clean condition with a fully inflated tyre to match is ideal. Being intended for field use only, an original jack should appear to have had little use. Any other breakdown equipment such as jump leads or warning triangles are a good sign of some forethought, but these may have already been removed for the sale.

Seats

The seats in all models are loved for their comfort which is still impressive even by today's standards. Available in cloth, part, or full leather depending on trim, the seats are hard wearing, with the best of the bunch being half leather. The cloth centres give to cope with years of use, and the leather trim and piping on the outer edges serve to reinforce and protect as people and objects enter and exit. Full cloth seats can sag in this area over time.

Seats should still be firm, so excessive sagging or a failed lumbar support will need replacement parts which are still available as new in some countries. Also don't forget to check that all seat adjustments and seat belts work as they should, and that there are no major marks, burns or tears in the seat material.

Some estates were fitted with an additional rear facing bench seat, increasing the capacity to seven people. They fold away well, but are really best suited for transporting children, who will no doubt enjoy waving at the drivers following you.

Carpet

As with the boot (trunk) check for any signs of water damage and investigate further by questioning the seller and lifting the carpet up if possible. Carpets tend to last really well and are securely installed. Heavy-duty plastic mats are a great additional feature if present.

Door cards

Front door cards offer plenty of storage by way of long, deep trays at the bottom of the front doors; these are divided into two sections on earlier models. Check these are still securely fastened.

The 'reach in and pull back to open' mechanism is very reliable compared to the average flap and rod system found in most cars, although later models did move on to use this system. If fitted, you may enjoy watching the occasional new passenger struggle with how to get out as they search for the familiar flap handle!

Leaning on the door card can dent it.

The indented trim panel often matches the seats. Check that this is also securely mounted. Immediately below this is a convenient place to rest one's elbow, so check this has not been dented as people lean on it to adjust their position in the seat.

Windows

All models were fitted with electric windows front and rear. The driver can operate all windows from the driver's control panel in the door, with the option to lock the rear windows from here if desired. In addition to this, rear windows only lower to around halfway to aid child safety. Child locks are also fitted to the rear doors as standard.

The driver's door control panel.

Another little safety detail.

Headlining

This is among the most common areas that fail with these cars; the headlining can sag over time as it loses adhesion with the roof card and the thin foam layer disintegrates. In most cases this will manifest only as a patch in the rear but is likely to get worse with time.

Replacing the lining is a simple DIY job, but it's time consuming to do

Replacing a sagging headlining is a time consuming task and you don't look up that often – so why not make it interesting!

properly. The brittle sculpted card, to which the lining is mounted, requires delicate hands to remove. If being undertaken on a saloon (sedan), it's highly advisable to remove the seats, or you'll be searching for an old rule and some duct tape to patch it up again after trying to bend it too far!

Sunroof

Available in manually wound or electric, the sunroofs are well designed with excellent rain water guttering. Unless the seals have failed, causing rust, you should only need to check the channels are all clean and unobstructed and that all the moving parts operate smoothly and as intended. Electric motors were known to fail after a lot of use and if strained by a stiff sliding mechanism, but replacement is a simple job. Replacement motors will become harder to find over time, however.

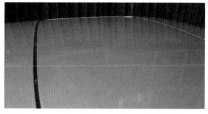
This sunroof is nice and straight, but the seal is starting to crack.

The sunroof framework needs to be kept clean for the drainage system to work properly.

Centre console & interior trim

Further to the headlining, another common area for failure is the top, padded area of the dashboard. Frequent exposure to hot sunlight has been known to cause many to crack.

Check the closure mechanism on the armrest lid of the centre console storage compartment, as heavy leaning on this at an angle can snap the male pin. Also look for any light carpet staining near the front of the console around the foot wells, as this could indicate a leaking heater matrix. You may also notice a slightly sweet smell if this is the case.

A quick check of the other interior trim pieces is worth your time. As with exterior trim, missing or damaged parts may not be expensive, but replacements of the correct type can be hard to find. Even then such parts often age

The rear ash tray can get kicked about and become loose.

A quirky modification turns the area under the radio into a miniature glove box.

differently. Check the plastic trim pieces around the framework, sills, seats, steering column, dashboard, mirrors and sun visors, ensuring all are secure and free of cracks and damage.

Gear stick (shifter)

Check that the various positions of the shifter engage correctly. Do so with the clutch down on manual examples. Engaging reverse on older models requires the lifting of a collar. Testing of the overdrive if fitted will have to wait until the test drive.

Instrument/gauge panel

The instrument panel is a standard affair; remember to check the functioning of each gauge and warning light when you get the engine running in the section to follow. Later models introduced a new shape of instrument panel to improve the layout of the gauges, making them more easily visible through the steering wheel. The turbo gauge on petrol turbo

Mk1 instrument clusters are just visible; who needs to look at the voltmeter and turbo gauge anyway?

models is not particularly accurate, more a guide as to correct function during spooling of the turbo. Remember also to check that the backlighting works and can be adjusted for brightness via the dial at the base of the instrument panel.

Pedals

Checking the pedals before starting the car is important and won't take a minute. The last thing you want to do is set off and then find one is loose, or worse still, not working. First, check the foot plates are securely fixed to the arms and have sufficient grip. Next, move the pedals laterally by hand to check for excessive play. Finally, check for full and smooth range of motion using your feet as if driving.

Starting & driving
Finally we're ready to start the car, examine how it drives, and test all those functions that require power or for the engine to be on. Each of the following sections describes any stationary checks first, followed by what to look for when driving. It's illegal to read a book while driving, so it's advisable to read the whole section first and make some notes!

Switches & controls

It may be tempting to switch the car on and test the operation of these immediately while the running engine can ensure you don't drain the battery. However, it is best to leave the testing of these to the end before you switch the engine off, as this will enable you to concentrate on how the engine starts from cold.

Once you've assessed this in the section below, ensure the car is in neutral and the handbrake on and working, before testing the electrical switches and controls.

This will allow you to safely exit and walk around the car as necessary while the engine is running. Ensure you are parked in a place where it is legal to do this. Methodically work your way from one area to another to ensure all functions are tested, noting down any failures or concerns as you do so.

Cold starting & engine tone

It's usually a good idea to have the bonnet (hood) open the first time you start the car. This will allow you to quickly spot any visual signs which could indicate problems; such as excessive vibrations, leaks or loose components. You can also get a much better idea of where in the engine bay any unusual knocks or noises are coming from should you hear any.

Carefully offer your hand up to the engine block or cam cover and check that the engine is cold. Ask the seller at this point when the car was last started; the fact that your checking anyway will encourage an honest answer.

If an engine has been running recently it will normally start more easily than if it was cold. The oil will be well circulated and the metal components

This bonnet (hood) pin needs a clean and re-grease.

expanded closer to operating temperature, meaning the engine will move more freely and thus be easier to start. Additionally the battery will have been recently topped up by the alternator and will therefore have maximum power for turning the engine over. If the battery has trouble holding charge this problem may not be exposed when performing a warm start.

Petrol engines in good working order should start within the first couple of seconds after turning the key. You can allow a little more time for diesels to start, especially in colder conditions, as the glow plugs take a moment to warm up. Once started, resist the urge to rev the engine immediately as it should be able to maintain idle without this input. If a couple of presses on the throttle are needed this isn't necessarily a bad thing, so long as idle can be maintained afterward.

Once the engine is at a comfortable idle speed, step out of the car and listen to the running tone, building some revs by manually operating the throttle from the engine bay. Here you can best detect any unusual noises. Refer back to Chapter 8 for engine specific information. Take any notes you may need and get a second opinion if unsure.

Lights

With the engine still at idle, once you have made any necessary notes about the cold start and checked the switches and controls, follow up with a quick check of all the lights. All models have daytime running lights, so don't be surprised that these are on when the engine is running – they should be. The headlights themselves vary in size and arrangement. For example European Volvos used E-Code headlamps with

Headlight washer-wipers come as standard, shown here on a European headlight.

a single main lens area, whereas US models predominantly used DOT headlamps with the main lens area divided into sections. These differing styles were abandoned in favour of universal sleeker headlights on later models. Aside from overall condition, ensure the headlights are free of condensation, securely attached, and correct for the side of the road you'll be driving on.

Testing the under bonnet (hood) light.

Further to the external lights, don't forget to check the following where fitted: boot (trunk) light – under-bonnet (hood) light – red door edge marker lights – rear seatbelt warning light – interior courtesy light – vanity mirror light – glove box light – ash tray light – cigarette lighter illumination.

Steering & handling

An initial amount of steering resistance after starting the engine is acceptable, but should quickly disappear to enable smooth operation of the steering wheel all the way to the locking point. It's normal to hear a squealing noise when hitting full lock, but this should be avoided, as it puts a strain on the steering pump. Any noise or resistance before this point, or if the steering cannot reach full lock, indicates a loose or worn belt, a worn steering pump, or not enough steering fluid (which could mean a leak).

With the road wheels back in straight ahead position, check to ensure the steering wheel is at zero degrees. In later 960s with an adjustable steering wheel, check the adjustable movement and ensure the steering isn't affected while set at its extreme ranges of motion. Set the steering at your desired position and move off.

When driving, take note of how the car behaves in a straight line at reasonable speed, how it reacts to different corners, and how it responds to changes between left and right steering input. There are various potential

Who needs an estate when you have a roof rack – although this may affect handling!

problems with steering and handling, and just as many potential causes. If you feel something isn't right with the way the car drives and can't identify it, an experienced friend or mechanic is invaluable. However, some possible issues and likely causes are discussed below.

A harsh ride where bumps in the road cause excessive jolting, or excessive leaning around corners, coupled with a slight loss of steering feel, is likely to be due to worn or broken suspension shocks. If the car feels like it flops from side to side when changing direction rather than maintaining the exact same course as the wheels, it may be that the anti-roll bar, panhard rod or suspension bushes are worn.

If the front wheels don't feel like they change direction in total unison when steering left and right, and there is a slight delay between the two of them being set on their new path, its likely that their tyres are unevenly worn, unevenly inflated, the steering joints worn, or the wheels misaligned. Swapping the front wheels over and experiencing the same effect can rule out the tyres although this is not usually practical on a test visit. Further examination once you return to a stand still can help to narrow the cause down.

If you experience the car pulling to the left or right this can also be down to the wheel alignment. A car will pull to the side that has the least caster and/or the most camber. Another potential cause of a car pulling to one side is the brakes.

Brake operation

After starting the car it would be normal to feel some release in the brake pedal resistance as the servo charges with air. However, the servo system is of an efficient design in these cars and pedal feel should revert to normal quickly. With the car still stationary, depress the brake pedal and hold it down to make sure there is no loss of resistance under a constant pressure. If there is, and the pedal continues to depress, it's likely there's a leak, and it would be advisable not to continue until this has been thoroughly checked out.

If the brakes just feel spongy, there is probably air in the fluid. It's normal for a small amount of air to build up in brake fluid over time. Proper bleeding of the system should eliminate the spongy feeling, and return the brakes to normal. Naturally, one should test the brakes at slow speed for feel and bite before moving off to drive. Also check the operation of the handbrake; the lever shouldn't move more than two inches to engage the parking brakes.

If experiencing wandering or pulling as described in the previous section, it could be down to two areas of the brakes. Seized or sticking callipers do not allow the pads to fully return to their resting position and it's this mild but constant application of the brakes that could cause the pulling over to the affected side. This is normally a call to replace the calliper, but if doing so it may be worth replacing the hoses first to rule that out. A collapsed brake hose may not be evident on external inspection, but the internal restriction can stop fluid returning back up the hose, leading to a constant pulling to one side.

If it's the case that the restriction in the brake hose merely delays the movement of fluid, this can be detected when braking. The car will move first to the unrestricted side, as this pad can reach it's disc first. This will be followed by a change in the direction of pull as the other brake catches up. If it's the front brakes that are affected, this motion is likely to be a small jerk. If the problem is at the rear, the car will be more gradually drawn from one side to the other.

Clutch & gearbox operation

A simple and assertive test for a clutch is not always popular, as it puts the engine under momentary stress, so ask the sellers' permission before performing the test.

With the engine running and ensuring there are no obstacles ahead,

Some flywheels are heavier than others.

shift into third gear and gradually release the clutch. If gripping properly the clutch should cause the engine to stall. If the engine continues running, the clutch will need replacing.

Another way to check the clutch is whilst driving. If revs increase suddenly when accelerating hard, it means the clutch is slipping, and can't grip at peak torque. If engine revs don't drop down normally between shifts, again, this means the clutch is worn, as it can't even resist the kinetic energy of the engine's rotating parts.

Automatic gearboxes should shift smoothly with very little noise. Jolts when actuating a new gear, or any unusual noises that cause concern, almost always indicate a worn transmission. You can also check the transmission oil which should be light and red in colour. If dark and burnt-smelling, this is a sign of wear and, at the very least, the oil should be changed.

Performance

Moving off from a stand still or slow speed, there should be no hesitation and power should be delivered smoothly and evenly through the middle rev range in each gear. If accelerating hard, the car should

The 531 cylinder head found on turbo models has the greatest flow rate of the 8v heads.

pull with an eagerness to match, especially 2.3 litre turbos where you should feel a noticeable surge as the turbo kicks in. On release of the throttle, the engine should decrease to more comfortable revs in the same smooth fashion.

Post-drive checks

Once stationary again, leave the car running and take note of the idle speed. It should be within the same parameters as when the car was started. A noticeably faster idle after warming up a carburetted engine indicates it was set too high to keep it running from cold and compensate for another problem.

Also check the engine temperature gauge, making sure it hasn't overheated. Now the engine is warm, engine fluids will be at a higher pressure, so once again check in the engine bay for any oil or water leaks and look under the car for drips.

Evaluation procedure

Add up the total points.

Score: 204 = excellent; 153 = good; 102 = average; 51 = poor. Cars scoring over 143 will be completely usable and will require only maintenance and care to preserve condition. Cars scoring between 51 and 104 will require some serious work (at much the same cost regardless of score). Cars scoring between 105 and 142 will require very careful assessment of the necessary repair/restoration costs in order to arrive at a realistic value.

10 Auctions
– sold! Another way to buy your dream

Auction pros & cons

Pros: Prices are usually lower than those of dealer or private sellers, and you might grab a real bargain on the day. Auctioneers have usually established clear title with the seller. At the venue you can usually examine documentation relating to the vehicle.

Cons: You have to rely on a sketchy catalogue description and history. The opportunity to inspect is limited, and you cannot drive the car. Auction cars are often a little below par and may require some work. It's easy to overbid. There will usually be a buyer's premium to pay in addition to the auction hammer price.

Which auction?

Auctions by established auctioneers are advertised in car magazines and on the auction houses' websites. A catalogue, or simple printed list of the lots for auctions might only be available a day or two ahead, though lots are normally listed and pictured on auctioneer websites much earlier. Contact the auction company to ask if previous auction selling prices are available, as this is useful information (details of past sales are often available on websites).

Catalogue, entry fee and payment details

When you purchase a catalogue of the vehicles in the auction, it often acts as a ticket allowing two people to attend the viewing days and auction. Catalogue details tend to be comparatively brief, but will include information such as 'one owner from new, low mileage, full service history', etc. It will also usually show a guide price to give you some idea of what to expect to pay and will tell you what is charged as a 'buyers premium'. The catalogue will also contain details of acceptable forms of payment. At the fall of a hammer an immediate deposit is usually required and the balance payable within 24 hours. If the plan is to pay cash, there may be a cash limit. Some auctions will accept payment by debit card. Sometimes credit or charge cards are acceptable, but will often incur an extra charge. A bank draft or bank transfer will have to be arranged in advance with your bank as well as with the auction house. No car will be released before all payments are cleared. If delays occur in payment transfers then storage costs can accrue.

Buyer's premium

A buyer's premium will be added to the hammer price: don't forget this in your calculations. It is not unusual for there to be a further state tax or local tax on the purchase price and/or the buyer's premium.

Viewing

In some instances it is possible to view on the day, or days before, as well as in the hours prior to, the auction. There are auction officials available who are willing to help out by opening engine and luggage compartments and to allow you to inspect the interior. While the officials may start the engine for you, a test drive is out of the question. Crawling under and around cars as much as you want is permitted, but you can't suggest that the car you're interested in be jacked up, or attempt to do the job yourself. You can also ask to see any documentation there is available.

Bidding

Before you take part in the auction, decide on your maximum bid – and stick to it!

It might take a while for the auctioneer to reach the lot you're interested in, so use that time to observe how other bidders behave. When it's the turn of your car, attract the auctioneers attention and make an early bid. The auctioneer will

First impressions of this 940 turbo are good, but a thorough examination at auction is not always possible.

then look to you for a reaction every time another bid is made; usually the bids will be in fixed increments until the bidding slows, when smaller increments will often be accepted before the hammer falls. If you want to withdraw from the bidding make sure the auctioneer understands your intentions – a vigorous shake of the head when he or she looks to you for the next bid should do the trick! Assuming that you are the successful bidder, the auctioneer will note your card or paddle number, and from that moment on you will be responsible for the vehicle.

If the car is unsold, either because it failed to reach the reserve or because there was little interest, it may be possible to negotiate with the owner, via the auctioneers, after the sale is over.

Successful bid

There are two items to think about. How to get the car home, and insurance. If you can't drive the car, your own or a hired trailer is one way, another is to have the vehicle shipped using the facilities of a local company. The auction house will also have details of companies specializing in the transfer of cars.

Insurance for immediate cover can usually be purchased on site, but it may be more cost effective to make arrangements with your own insurance company in advance, and then call them to confirm full details.

eBay & other online auctions

eBay and other online auctions could land you a car at a bargain price, though you'd be foolhardy to bid without examining the car first, something most vendors encourage. A useful feature of eBay is that the geographical location of the vehicle is shown, so you can narrow your choices to those within a realistic radius of home. Be prepared to outbid in the last few moments of the auction. A stopwatch can be useful to time your final highest bid down to the last few sections, leaving next to no time for other bidders to respond; that is of course unless you have already been

A successful bid on the right car will lead to a very fulfilling journey home.
(Courtesy Dustin Hulting)

outbid! If you see an example of interest that has received no bids, try to decide if it looks appealing to someone on the hunt for a bargain who's not necessarily out to find this particular model, as you are. If you believe this to be the case, it can often be beneficial to place the initial bid to put such bargain hunters off. If they bid first and are outbid by you, they may get stubborn and pay more than they planned to or push your bid up. Remember your bid is binding and it will be very, very difficult to get restitution in the case of a crooked vendor fleecing you – caveat emptor!

Be aware that some cars offered for sale in online auctions are 'ghost' cars. Don't part with any cash without being sure that the vehicle does actually exist and is as described (usually a pre-bidding inspection is possible).

Auctioneers
Barrett-Jackson www.barrett-jackson.com
Bonhams www.bonhams.com
British Car Auctions (BCA) www.bca-europe.com or www.british-carauctions.co.uk
Cheffins www.cheffins.co.uk
Christies www.christies.com
Coys www.coys.co.uk
eBay www.eBay.com
H&H www.classic-auctions.co.uk
RM www.rmauctions.com
Shannons www.shannons.com.au
Silver www.silverauctions.com

11 Paperwork
– correct documentation is essential!

The paper trail

Classic, collector and prestige cars usually come with a large portfolio of paperwork accumulated and passed on by a succession of proud owners. This documentation represents the real history of the car, and from it can be deduced the level of care the car has received, how much it's been used, which specialists have worked on it, and the dates of major repairs and restorations. All of this information will be priceless to you as the new owner, so be very wary of cars with little paperwork to support their claimed history.

Registration documents

All countries/states have some form of registration for private vehicles, whether it's like the American 'pink slip,' or the British 'log book' systems.

It's essential to check that the registration document is genuine, that it relates to the car in question, and that all the vehicle's details are correctly recorded, including chassis/VIN and engine numbers (if these are shown). If you are buying from the previous owner, his or her name and address will be recorded in the document: this will not be the case if you are buying from the dealer.

The storage area in the rear armrest can be a great place to keep handbooks and notes you don't need often.

In the UK, the current (Euro-aligned) registration document is named 'VC5,' and is printed in coloured sections of blue green and pink. The blue section relates to the car specification, the green section has details of the new owner and the pink section is sent to the DVLA in the UK when the car is sold. A small section in yellow deals with selling the car within the motor trade.

In the UK, the DVLA will provide details of earlier keepers of the vehicle upon payment of a small fee, and much can be learned in this way.

If the car has a foreign registration there may be expensive and time-consuming formalities to complete. Do you really want the hassle?

44

Roadworthiness certificate

Most country/state administrators require that vehicles are regularly tested to prove that they are safe to use on the public highway and do not produce excessive emissions. In the UK, that test (the 'MoT') is carried out at approved testing stations, for a fee. In the USA, the requirement varies, but most states insist on an emissions test every two years as a minimum, while the police are charged with pulling over unsafe-looking vehicles.

In the UK, the test is required on an annual basis, once a vehicle becomes three years old. Of particular relevance for older cars; does the certificate issued include the mileage reading at the test date and, therefore, become an independent record of that car's history? Ask the dealer if previous certificates are available. Without an MoT, the vehicle should be trailered to its new home, unless you insist that a valid MoT is part of the deal. (Not such a bad idea, as at least you will know the car was roadworthy on the day it was tested and you don't need to wait for the older certificate to expire before having the test done.)

Road licence

The administration of every country/state charges some kind of tax for the use of it's road system, with the actual form of the 'road licence' and how it is displayed, varying enormously country to country and state to state.

Whatever the form of the 'road licence', it must relate to the vehicle carrying it and must be present and valid if the car is to be driven on the public highway legally. The value of the licence will depend on the length of time it will continue to be valid. In the UK, if a car is untaxed because it has not been used for a period of time, the owner has to inform the licensing authorities, otherwise the vehicles date-related registration number will be lost and there will be a painful amount of paperwork to get it re-registered. Also in the UK, vehicles built before the end of 1972 are provided with 'tax discs' free of charge, but they must still display a valid disc. Car clubs can often provide formal proof that a particular car qualifies for this valuable concession.

Certificates of authenticity

For many makes of collectible car it is possible to get a certificate proving the age and authenticity (eg engine and chassis numbers, paint colour and trim) of a particular vehicle. These are sometimes called 'Heritage Certificates' and if the car comes with one of these it is a definite bonus. If you want to obtain one, the relevant owners' club is the best starting point.

If the car has been used in European classic car rallies it may have a FIVA (Federation Internationale des Vehicules Anciens) certificate. The so-called 'FIVA Passport,' or 'FIVA Vehicle Identity Card,' enables organisers and participants to recognise whether or not a particular vehicle is suitable for individual events. If you want to obtain such a certificate go to www.fbhvc.co.uk or www.fiva.org. There will be similar organisations in other countries.

Valuation certificate

Hopefully, the vendor of a collectible car will have a recent valuation certificate, or letter signed by a recognised expert stating how much he, or she, believes the particular car to be worth (such documents, together with photos, are usually needed to get 'agreed value' insurance). Generally, such documents should act only as confirmation of your own assessment of the car rather than a guarantee of value as the expert has probably not seen the car in the flesh. The easiest way to find out how to obtain a formal valuation is to contact one of the specialist organizations listed in chapter 16.

Service history
Often these cars will have been serviced at home by enthusiastic (and hopefully capable) owners for a good number of years. Nevertheless, try to obtain as much service history and other paperwork pertaining to the car as you can. Naturally, dealer stamps, or specialist garage receipts, score most points in the value stakes. However, anything helps in the great authenticity game – items like the original bill of sale, handbook, parts invoices and repair bills, add to the story and character of the car. Even a brochure correct to the year of the car's manufacture is a useful document, and something that you could well have to search hard for in future years. If the seller claims that the car has been restored, expect receipts and other evidence from a specialist restorer.

Similarly, if the seller claims to have carried out regular servicing, ask what work was completed, and when, and seek some evidence of it being done. Your assessment of the car's overall condition should tell you whether the seller's claims are genuine.

Restoration photographs
If the seller tells you that the car has been restored, then expect to be shown a series of photographs taken while the restoration was under way. Pictures taken at various stages, and from various angles, should help you gauge the thoroughness of the work. If you buy the car, ask if you can have all the photographs, as they form an important part of the vehicle's history. It's surprising how many sellers are happy to part with their car and accept your cash, but want to hang on to their photographs! In the latter event, you may be able to persuade the vendor to get a set of copies made.

A comprehensive service history is always a welcome sight.

12 What's it worth?
– let your head rule your heart

Condition

If the example you've been looking at hasn't met expectations during the 15 minute evaluation it is unlikely you will have used the marking system in chapter 9, but hopefully viewing it will have provided you with some useful experience.

If your candidate has reached the marking stage, however, you'll have built up a pretty good picture of the car's condition, and now need to make a judgement about value.

Compare the findings from your evaluation of the car to the value listings in this book, those available in magazines, and online. Bear in mind the cost and time of any work or repairs that will need doing, and use real selling price data – from eBay for example – that gives your offer credibility. Some owners may not realise how much their car has depreciated, or the time and expense involved in putting faults right. Use your recently acquired knowledge to persuade them and get the best price. For example, these large cars are popularly misconceived as 'gas guzzlers,' so the seller may even be downsizing to save money: a point which could work in your favour. Identifying any non-standard features of the car and determining if they add to, or detract from, its value can also be useful. Find out what to look for below.

Desirables

As with most makes of car, the desirable features that normally add value are more likely found in later models and higher trim levels. However, this depends entirely on what you're looking for. For example, if you prefer the stronger lines of the earlier shape 700s you'll be missing out on some of the features included on the later, sleeker models, such as the improved Bosch Jetronic engine management. Models fitted with the V6 engines are

Original heavy-duty floor mats are a plus.

likely to have more optional extras, but if you're looking for better fuel economy or want to modify, the four-cylinder Red Block uses less fuel in standard form, and power is more easily increased.

The cream full leather interior in this 960 exudes luxury.

47

Turbo models (both diesel and petrol) are generally more sought after.

Undesirables

A well-used tow bar means the car is likely to have done some pulling. Most models are more than capable of this, but the added weight may have prematurely caused the rear suspension springs to sag.

An all-blue interior is not to everyone's taste, but it does have a retro feel.

While generally trouble free, carburettors, as fitted on some models, have become outdated. Found only on earlier models, where rust can also be an issue, they require more adjustment and are generally down on power compared to the later injection models.

Some aftermarket additions are less suitable than others.

The all-blue seat cloth and trim available on some models is not to everyone's taste. Any modifications that are not in keeping with the aesthetics of the car, such as elaborate chromed wheels, are not desirable selling points.

Sealing the deal

Unless you're buying through an auction, the seller will normally expect an offer below the asking price. Having completed your research and examined the vehicle thoroughly, you'll be well positioned to negotiate based on the cost of any work that needs doing, and benefits that may have been oversold.

If you have any reservations causing you to push for a price the seller won't accept, they may be receptive to you meeting their bottom line, subject to an independent mechanical inspection.

13. Do you really want to restore?

– it'll take longer and cost more than you think

The age of these vehicles means that they're not likely to be considered for restoration in the conventional sense, despite there being examples from as far back as 1982. Popular as family cars or load luggers, well cared for, or workhorses, there are plenty of examples to choose from in terms of condition. Quite frankly, aside from aesthetic touch ups, 700/900 Series Volvos either work or they don't. If it takes anything more than a little work to get one running, then it's been intentionally thrashed into permanent submission.

However, when fixing problems, it's good to know that numerous Volvo parts from different models can fit. And this is where the fun starts, as with a little research you'll often find you can upgrade the part you needed to replace with a later variant. For example, M90 gearboxes from later models can be fitted to earlier cars, using the clutch from diesel models. But whether

The 16v head can be used in conjunction with a Red Block (painted blue here), and a large turbo for enjoyable results!

you're intending to just bring a Volvo back to its peak, or planning some extensive modifications, there are a few factors to consider.

Difficulty

The first thing to consider is if you are able to complete the project on your own, or if you will need help. In fact, no matter how much experience you have, you're likely to need help at some point, however little. It could be simply asking a question on a forum,

Modest handling and brake upgrades are fairly easy to do, and essential when upping the power.

employing the services of a knowledgeable friend, or even just someone strong enough to lift something with you. Research is key; if you know exactly what you need to do before you start, you won't be entering into something you might not be able to finish!

Time

If you're fitting the project in around a full time job, be realistic about how much time you really have available in a day. By the time you've changed in and out of some old clothes, brought out your tools and packed everything away again, this will be less time than you expected. If considering anything more than a few routine jobs, however long you think the project will take, double it. If you complete everything in record time, you'll be grateful for the extra time to tinker, and this will also mean more time for that all important test drive.

Stripping the car till it resembles an aircraft fuselage will involve a lot of time.

Money

For all but a minority of pockets, the scope of restoration and modifications is ultimately limited by how much money you have to spend. Be realistic and consider everything; replacement gaskets, fluids, and nuts and bolts all add up. Furthermore, you're not likely to see anything other than a financial loss if you sell the car, but that's not why you're doing it is it?

Planning

Having considered the basics above, if you're now ready to get stuck into creating that satisfying end result, you'll need to do some planning. Do you have all the tools you'll need? Will you be affected by the weather or seasons? How much space do you require, and how long will you realistically be able to use that space? What if the project gets delayed? Thorough planning will ensure a much more enjoyable project and doubtless a more satisfying end result.

14 Paint problems
– bad complexion, including dimples, pimples and bubbles

Paint faults generally occur due to lack of protection, maintenance, or poor preparation prior to a respray or touch-up. Some of the following conditions may be present in the car you're looking at.

Orange peel
This appears as an uneven paint surface similar in appearance to the skin of an orange. The fault is caused by the failure of atomised paint droplets to flow into each other when they hit the surface. It's sometimes possible to rub

Clear weather and good daylight will either show off good paintwork or reveal problems.

out the effect with proprietary paint cutting/rubbing compound or very fine grades of abrasive paper. A respray may be necessary in severe cases. Consult a bodywork repairer/paint shop for advice.

Cracking
Severe cases are likely to have been caused by too heavy an application of paint (or filler beneath the paint). Also, insufficient stirring of the paint before application can lead to the components being improperly mixed, and cracking can result. Incompatibility with the paint already on the panel can have a similar effect. To rectify it is necessary to rub down to a smooth, sound finish before respraying the problem area.

Crazing
Sometimes the paint takes on a crazed rather than a cracked appearance when the problems mentioned under 'cracking' are present. This problem can also be caused by a reaction between the underlying surface and the paint. Paint removal and respraying the problem area is usually the only solution.

Blistering
Almost always caused by corrosion of the metal beneath the paint. Usually perforation will be found in the metal, and the damage will normally be worse than that suggested by the area of blistering. The metal will have to be repaired before repainting. Micro blistering is usually the result of an economy respray, where inadequate heating has allowed moisture to settle on the vehicle before spraying. Consult a paint specialist, but damaged paint will have to be removed before partial or full respraying. This condition can also be caused by car covers that don't 'breathe.'

Fading

Some colours, especially reds, are prone to fading if subjected to strong sunlight for long periods without the benefit of polish protection. Sometimes, proprietary paint restorers and/or paint cutting/rubbing compounds will retrieve the situation. Often, a respray is the only real solution.

Peeling

Often a problem with metallic paintwork when the sealing lacquer becomes damaged and begins to peel off. Poorly applied paint may also peel. The remedy is to strip and start again.

Dimples

Dimples in the paintwork are caused by the residue of polish (particularly silicone types) not being removed properly before respraying. Paint removal and repainting is the only solution.

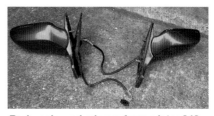

Body-coloured mirrors from a later 940 – be sure they have colour-aged the same as the body if buying replacements.

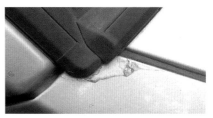

Peeling lacquer is common here where water pools at the base of the windscreen frame.

Dents

Small dents are usually easily cured by the 'Dentmaster,' or equivalent process, that sucks or pushes out the dent (as long as the paint surface is still intact). Companies offering dent removal services usually come to your home: consult your telephone directory or the internet.

Galvanized steel protects for years, even when the metal is bare.

15 Problems due to lack of use

– just like their owners, Volvos need exercise!

When considering buying a car, one of the first things that many people look at is the number of miles it has covered. There's usually a figure for most cars that would cause you to question how much life there is left in it – and whether it's worth purchasing – having reached that many miles. However, mileage is not the whole story. If a car has not covered many miles, it may have only been used for short journeys, which is never good for an engine as it doesn't give it time to properly warm up before being switched off again. The constant demands of starting and stopping increase wear further. With all 700/900 engines capable of over 300,000 miles, this emphasizes the point that the condition and service history of the car are more important than the number of miles its covered.

Cold weather can be even harder on cars used for short journeys only.

Worse than short journeys however, is not being used at all. If a car has not been used for a long period of time, a proper laying up procedure should be carried out. This includes things as simple as lifting all wiper blades off the glass, relieving the pressure on the static rubber, which would otherwise harden in its current shape and stick to the glass, rendering it useless. Very few car owners employ such preparations when leaving a vehicle unused. Some of the other consequences and preventative measures are outlined below.

Seized components
Over time, pistons and the big ends of engines can become seized due to corrosion. In the shorter term, oil residue can thicken around engine internals, causing starting troubles. Removing the sparkplugs and spraying a small amount of clean oil onto the combustion chambers helps to prevent seizing. The engine can be turned by hand with the plugs out (in neutral gear). Doing this every two months will help keep the engine moving freely when not in use.

The pistons in brake and clutch (if hydraulic) components can seize after long periods without use. Clean these with an approved brake cleaner, rinse and dry them off, and use a silicone-based lubricant. WD-40 should be avoided here as, contrary to popular belief, it is not a lubricant, merely an effective cleaning agent and water dispersant. In this case it would break down dirt, potentially washing it into the moving parts we're trying to protect. Silicone lubricants not only lubricate, but help to condition and preserve rubber components. Just be sure not to get any on the brake pads as this will ruin them!

If left on, handbrakes can seize. Leave the car in gear with the handbrake off and chock the wheels if necessary.

Door locks can also seize. Place a small amount of oil on the door key and insert it into the lock to coat the internals.

Fluids

Empty space in a fuel tank can allow condensation to form and corrode the tank from the inside. Fill the tank to the top to minimize space in which this could occur. If leaving the car for over six months it's recommended that a fuel stabilizer is added, as fuel can go stale.

Some additives in engine oil are slightly caustic and can cause damage after long periods of time. Change the oil before storing the car and enquire about additive free oils for long-term use.

Engine coolant can freeze in winter, expanding to cause cracks in the engine. Ensure the correct amount of anti-freeze has been added. Most brands also include corrosion protection.

Brake fluid absorbs water over time which can cause corrosion. Change brake fluid every two-three years.

Battery & electrical

Even with the engine switched off, most cars maintain some draw from the battery which can go flat in the absence of a running engine to charge it. Ensure you know your stereo and any security codes before disconnecting the battery. Use a dielectric grease to protect terminals, connections and earthing points.

This wiring jacket has split after losing flexibility because the door has remained closed for a long period.

Tyres & rubber

Tyres can harden, crack and lose shape when left static under the weight of a vehicle. Air contracting over time can allow a flat spot to develop where the tyres are pressed against the ground. A temporary solution is to slightly over inflate the tyres. Longer term, jacking the car up will alleviate the problem but this isn't kind to suspension which is designed to be under stress. Some people remove their good wheels and leave the car on 'junk' wheels. Rubber dressing sprays are available but silicone lubricant works just as well.

Aside from tyres many other rubber components can harden, crack and perish – silicone spray helps here, too.

Windscreen wiper rubber loses elasticity over time.

Corrosion

WD-40 can help protect the non-moving metal parts of the car from corrosion. Aluminium engine components are particularly vulnerable.

Exhaust gasses naturally contain water. With regular use, the moisture is suspended in the warm exhaust gases and continually carried out. Lack of use will allow this moisture to settle, condensing and rusting the exhaust from the inside. Volvo exhausts are pretty resilient, but stainless replacement exhausts will suffer much less.

General

Without regular use, moisture gets easily trapped inside a car's interior which can foul electrics, gauges and allow mould and mildew to accumulate on carpets, upholstery and leather. Leaving the windows open a crack (if there is low risk of theft) aids ventilation to interiors, while moisture absorbers can help to keep things dry.

Debris collecting due to lack of use stops drainage and retains water, causing corrosion.

A plastic moisture barrier on the ground also prevents rising vapour to minimize condensation.

Small animals and insects can get into to any holes left unattended. Rodents can chew wiring and hoses and insects can block up air filters. Covering these areas and plugging holes such as the exhaust can dissuade unwanted intruders. Remember to keep note of all the measurements you've taken, for reference when the car undergoes de-preservation in the future.

Protection against damp is needed when interiors are left without the natural ventilation of driving.

16 The Community
– key people, organisations and companies in the Volvo world

The Volvo community is among the most enthusiastic and helpful to be found anywhere. You're likely to forget what you were doing before the conversion started when you discover someone is another Volvo enthusiast. Part of the reason for this is that the community is fairly small, and so it's rather rare to find a like-minded devotee to the 'prancing moose' (apart from in Sweden of course!). In the UK at least, Volvos of the era concerned here sometimes suffer a bit of a stigma for being boxy and uninteresting. This, coupled with its size, means the community tends to stick together, confident in coming to the defence of the marquee should such banter ensue.

Your author, right, with Alan Beavis and his 1988 740 Turbo Intercooler.

Owners have frequently been brought up with Volvos in the family before purchasing their own, and you'll often find 'partisans' with many loyal years of ownership. This is another great aspect to the community. Wives and girlfriends complain as much as any other car enthusiasts' partners, should you forget all else and spend an entire day in the garage. However, deep down, they still hold an affection of their own for the cosy Volvo, safe in the knowledge that there's at least one reliable member of the family!

If you go in search of information you can't do much better than one of

'If more people drove Volvos - there'd be more people' – the smaller 460 from the same era protected its driver in an accident, who walked away with just a scratch.

the main Volvo forums. There are groups of enthusiasts in virtually every market the cars were sold in. However, turbobricks.com and volvoforums.org.uk are among those with the greatest wealth of information. If you've searched thoroughly within previous forum posts but still can't find an answer to your question, there's usually no end of people willing to try and help. A list of major clubs and resources follows below.

Clubs

UK: Volvo Owners' club, Volvo Performance Club UK, Volvo Enthusiasts Club
USA:Turbobricks (US/UK), Volvo Club of America (VCOA), Volvo Sports America
Australia:The Volvo Owners' club of NSW, Swedishbrick Car Club of Australia (SCCA), The Volvo Club of Victoria, Volvo Club of Queensland
Canada: Canadian Volvo Club
South Africa: Volvo Owners' club of South Africa
Norway: Norwegian Volvo Club.

Websites

UK
www.volvoforums.org.uk
www.vpcuk.org
http://volvoenthusiastsclub.co.uk
http://forums.t5d5.org/
USA
www.turbobricks.com
www.vcoa.org
http://forums.swedespeed.com/forum.php
http://www.vsa.org/
www.matthewsvolvosite.com
www.volvoforums.com
Australia
http://www.downunderbricks.com/blog/

http://www.volvoclubqld.org.au/
http://www.volvocarclubnsw.com/
www.volvovic.org.au
Canada
www.canadianvolvoclub.org
South Africa
www.volvoclub.co.za
Norwaywww.norskvolvoklubb.no/
Sweden
www.swedishbrick.org
Drifting:
www.driftworks.com
www.drift.com www.driftlock.co.uk

Magazines

Volvo Driver (Volvo Owners' Club magazine) - *Rolling magazine* (Volvo Club of America) – *Rolling Magazine* (Volvo Club of Victoria – Australia) - *Classic Car Magazine* (UK) - *Classic and Sports Car Magazine* (UK) – Teknikens Varld (Sweden)

A far Eastern Volvo looking quite at home in the snow.

17 Vital statistics
– essential data at your fingertips

700 Series
Produced: 1982-1992
Approx' production volumes:

740.. 1,000,000
760.. 220,000
780.. 8500

TOTAL:
1,228,500

Trim levels available: 760 GLE, GLE Turbo Diesel, Turbo - 740 GL, GLE, GLT 16V,
GLE Turbo Diesel, Turbo, SE - 780 Bertone Coupé

900 Series
Produced: 1990 –1998
Approx' production volumes:

940.. 480,000
960.. 150,000
S90 52,000
V90 18,000

TOTAL:
700,000

Trim levels available: 960 GLT, SE - 940 GL, GLE, Turbo, SE - S90 GLT, SE - V90
GLT, SE

With so many combinations of engine, power and trim, the information on the
opposite page is not a complete list, but provides a comprehensive overview.

Year	Model	Trim	Engine	BHP	Torque (Nm)	Weight (kg)	Top speed (mph)	0-60mph (secs)
1983	740	GLE	2.0L	131	190	1269	112	9.8
1984 on	740	GL	2.3L	113	192	1250	111	11.8
1984 on	760	GLE Auto	2.8L	154	234	1325	114	–
1984 on	760	GLE	2.8L	154	234	1303	118	9.3
1984 on	740	Turbo	2.3L	180	260	1330	124	8
1984 on	760	Turbo Diesel	2.4L	110	194	1420	109	11.8
1985 on	740	GL cat	2.3L	111	185	1290	109	11.3
1985-88	780	Turbo	2.5L	163	250	1420	124	9.5
1985-88	780	Turbo Diesel	2.4L	121	240	1470	115	9.9
1985-88	780	V6	2.8L	145	235	1420	112	11.2
1986 on	740	Kombi GL	2.3L	113	192	1330	106	11.1
1986 on	740	Kombi GLE	2.3L	129	190	1336	114	9.9
1988	780	Turbo 16V	2.0L	197	290	1569	132	8.2
1989	740	GLT 16V	2.3L	155	203	1372	124	8.5
1990	960	GL	2.3L	165	263	1524	123	9.7
1990	960	24v	2.9L	201	267	1524	128	9.3
1990	960	Turbo	2.3L	190	279	1407	127	8.9
1990	940	S	2.0L	111	157	1372	111	13.2
1990	940	SE	2.0L	155	233	1402	124	9.3
1990	940	2.3	2.3L	155	203	1417	124	10.3
1997	S90	24v	2.9L	178	260	1543	130	8.8

The Essential Buyer's Guide™ series ...

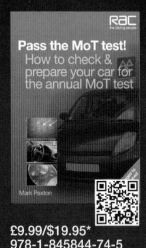

Index